MW01600330

Foreword

Jaap Sahib was composed by the tenth Guru, Guru Gobind Singh.

Jaap Sahib is composed of 199 *pauris* or verses, in the form of rhymed couplets and the vocabulary is superb.

Jaap Sahib is a total and complete introduction to a non-individual Creator (God), or Nature itself. The verses are in the form of rhymed couplets and the vocabulary and ingenuity are superb.

The immortal One is far beyond human comprehension, and Guru Gobind Singh has gracefully presented a composition for one to get an insight into the Supreme Being.

Jaap Sahib is a rhythmic hymn, composed like a necklace with pearls and jewels beautifully arranged around a string (the string refers to the Supreme God); the pearls and jewels are His attributes, virtues, and glories.

Jaap Sahib is an introduction to God. The glories sung (composed) by Guru Gobind Singh revolve around the following attributes of God:

1

God is metaphysical, beyond time, Eternal, Unborn, not created, Self-existent, and without form, feature, color or contour. Therefore, neither can He be described or depicted, nor can anyone make His image or idol.

God is Universal, pervading in all of His manifestations. He cannot be confined to any particular place, land, country, religion, race, body or name.

God is the Creator of the Universe and the laws governing it. His Law and Justice is Righteous and Ultimate.

God is pervasive in His Creation and also extends beyond it; He is thus engrained in His Creation and at the same time transcends it. God is Omnipotent, Omnipresent, and omniscient. Nothing can happen outside of His Will; whether good or evil, He is the Creator-Sustainer-Destroyer of His Creation. He Himself is the Life of life, the Death of death. He is the Darkness of darkness, the Light of light.
THANK YOU GOD

Copyright © 2014
ISBN-13:978-1500417161
ISBN-10:1500417165

Jaap Sahib Translation

God is One, and can be realized by the grace of a true Guru.

JAAP
Uttered by the Tenth Guru (Guru Gobind Singh Ji)

Chhapai Chhand (Name of Verses), ***Tav Prasad*** (uttered with God's Grace).
God has no mark, color, caste or lineage.
No one can describe His shape, color, complexion and outline.
He is eternal, self-illuminated, and his power is beyond measure.
God is the King of kings, and the God of millions of Indras (Lord of weather).
God is the Emperor of the three worlds (of everything), demigods, men and demons; and He is proclaimed as indiscernible.
No one can relate all the Names of God, who is referred to by special Names, according to His excellences and doings. -1-

Bhujang Prayat Chhand (Name of Verses)
I salute the Immortal God.
I salute the Merciful God.
I salute the Formless God.
I salute God, Who is without a parallel. -2-

I salute God, Who has no dress.
I salute God, Who is beyond description.
I salute God, Who has no body.

I salute God, Who was not born. -3-

I salute God, Who cannot be conquered.
I salute God, Who cannot be destroyed.
I salute God, Who has no particular name.
I salute God, Who has no particular place. -4-

I salute God, Who is above all rituals, and Who is not bound to any work.
I salute God, Who is above formal observances.
I salute God, Who has no special name.
I salute God, Who has no particular home. -5-

I salute God, Who cannot be conquered.
I salute God, Who is not afraid of anyone.
I salute God, Who is unshakable.
I salute God, Who cannot be overthrown. -6-

I salute God, Who has no color or form.
I salute God, Who has no beginning.
I salute God, Who is unbreakable.
I salute God, Who is unfathomable. -7-

I salute God, Who is invincible.
I salute God, Who cannot be destroyed.
I salute God, Who is big hearted.
I salute God, Who is boundless. -8-

I salute God, Who is One.
I salute God, Who has many manifestations.
I salute God, Who is not made of the elements.
I salute God, Who is free from all entanglements. -9-

I salute God, Who is above rituals and has no engagements.
I salute God, Who is free from doubts,
I salute God, Who does not belong to any region.
I salute God, Who has no dress. -10-

I salute God, Who has no particular name.
I salute God, Who has no desires.
I salute God, Who is beyond the elements.
I salute God, Who cannot be injured. -11-

I salute God, Who is immovable.
I salute God, Who is not made from the five elements.
I salute God, Who is invisible.
I salute God, Who has no worries. -12-

I salute God, Who is above all troubles.
I salute God, Who cannot be installed.
I salute God, Who is cherished by all.
I salute God, Who is the real Treasure. -13-

I salute God, Whose depth is unknown.
I salute God, Who is unshakable.
I salute God, Who is the source of the three supreme virtues.
I salute God, Who cannot be created. -14-

I salute God, Who cherishes all.
I salute God, Who is omnipresent.
I salute God, Who has no color.
I salute God, Who cannot be destroyed. -15-

I salute God, Who is incomprehensible.

I salute God, Who is most beautiful.
I salute God, Who pervades oceans.
I salute God, Who needs no help. -16-

I salute God, Who has no caste.
I salute God, Who has no dynasty.
I salute God, Who has no religion.
I salute God, Who is wonderful. -17-

I salute God, Who does not belong to any particular
place.
I salute God, Who wears no dress.
I salute God, Who has no particular home.
I salute God, Who is unborn and unaffected by
mammon. -18-

I salute God, Who causes all to die.
I salute God, Who shows mercy to all.
I salute God, Who is present in all beings.
I salute God, Who is the Emperor of all. -19-

I salute God, Who is the destroyer of all.
I salute God, Who creates all.
I salute God, Who kills all.
I salute God, Who cares for all. -20-

I salute God, Who is the Light in all.
I salute God, Whose secrets cannot be known.
I salute God, Who is unborn.
I salute God, Who is most beautiful. -21-

I salute God, Who can reach all.
I salute God, Who resides everywhere.

I salute God, Who is the creator of all colors.
I salute God, Who is the destroyer of all. -22-

I salute God, Who can destroy death itself.
I salute God, Who is the fountain of mercy.
I salute God, Who is indescribable.
I salute God, Who never dies. -23-

I salute God, Who never becomes old.
I salute God, Who creates all.
I salute God, Who accomplishes everything.
I salute God, Who is free from all restrictions. -24-

I salute God, Who has no relatives.
I salute God, Who is not afraid of anybody.
I salute God, Who is merciful.
I salute God, Who bestows gifts. -25-

I salute God, Who is unlimited.
I salute God, Who is the greatest of all.
I salute God, Who loves all.
I salute God, Who is the highest. -26-

I salute God, Who annihilates all.
I salute God, Who nurtures all.
I salute God, Who creates all.
I salute God, Who destroys all. -27-

I salute God, Who is the highest Yogi (Holy person).
I salute God, Who is the biggest family-man.
I salute God, Who shows mercy to all.
I salute God, Who takes care of all. -28-

Chachri Chhand (*Name of Verses*), **Tav Prasad** (*uttered with God's Grace*).
God has no form.
God has no parallel.
God is immovable.
God does not take birth. -29-

God cannot be described.
God has no dress.
God has no particular name.
God has no desires. -30-

God is beyond the comprehension of the human mind.
God's secrets cannot be known.
God cannot be conquered.
God is not afraid of anybody.-31-

God is worshipped in the three worlds (everywhere).
God is the Supreme Treasure.
God is the fountain of gifts.
God was never born. -32-

God is without color.
God's origin is unknown.
God never gets old.
God is free from transmigration (birth and death). -33-

God was not born.
God has no color or caste.
God is above all elements.
God does not need anybody to nurture Him. -34-

God cannot be conquered.
God cannot be injured.
None can fight God.
God is unshakable -35-

God is very deep (unfathomable).
God is the friend of all.
God is free from all entanglements.
God is free from all bondage.-36-

God cannot be known.
God is beyond human comprehension.
God is free from death.
God is beyond the reach of mammon. -37-

God cannot be found.
God has no special abode.
God is boundless.
God is the greatest of all. -38-

God cannot be described.
God has no relatives.
God needs no support.
God cannot be understood. -39-

God is beyond reach.
God is unborn.
God is above the elements.
God is not tangible -40-

God cannot be seen.
God is free from worries.

God is beyond rites.
God has no doubts. -41-

God cannot be conquered.
God has no fear.
God is steady.
God's depth cannot be known.-42-

God cannot be measured or weighed.
God is the treasure of all.
God has countless forms.
Yet God has no form. -43-

Bhujang Prayat Chhand
Salutations to God, Who is respected by all.
Salutations to God, Who is the treasure of everything.
Salutations to God, Who is above all the gods.
God has no dress and is a mystery. -44-

Salutations to God, Who can destroy death.
Salutations to God, Who nurtures all.
Salutations to God, Who can reach all places.
Salutations to God, Who is present everywhere. -45-

God, Who is Master of all, has no body.
No one is equal to God.
Salutations to God, Who is the Sun of suns.
Salutations to God, Who is respected by all. -46-

Salutations to God, Who gives light to the moon.
Salutations to God, Who gives light to the sun.
Salutations to God, Who is the creator of music.

Salutations to God, Who is the creator of different tunes. -47-

Salutations to God, Who makes others dance.
Salutations to God, Who is the creator of sounds.
Salutations to God, Who beats the drums.
Salutations to God, Who enacts the worldly drama. -48-

Salutations to God, Who has no body, or name.
Salutations to God, Whose beauty is present in all.
God alone can cause the end of creation.
God is the provider of spiritual and miraculous powers. -49-

God is free and God is pure.
Salutations to God, Who is the king of kings, and highest of the high. -50-

Salutations to God, Who wields swords and other weapons.
Salutations to God, Who can launch arrows and other weapons. -51-

Salutations to God, Who knows everything.
Salutations to God, Who loves the world like a mother. -52-

God has no dress, and is free from doubts and temptations.
Salutations to God, Who is the Yogi (Holy Man) of Yogis (Holy Men). -53-

Salutations to God, Who protects all, and sets right the evil doer.
Salutations to God, Who nurtures all, including the virtuous and evil, as well as the spirits. -54-

Salutations to God, Who kills diseases, and is the essence of love.
Salutations to God, Who is the Emperor of emperors. -55-
Salutations to God, Who is the biggest donor, and the most respectable.
Salutations to God, Who cures all diseases, restores health, and washes sins. -56-

Salutations to God, Whose Name is the greatest magical word.
Salutations to God, Whose Name is the true amulet and charm.
God is the Supreme object of worship.
God (God's Name) is the greatest charm. -57-

God is the fountain of truth, peace and pleasure and can destroy all.
No one is bigger than God, Who is present everywhere.-58-

God is the giver of Spiritual power, Wisdom and Success.
God is present in the nether regions, the skies and space; and is the destroyer of all sins. -59-

God gives success and spiritual power, and is understanding. -60-

God, the Greatest Master, nurtures all without being seen.
God cannot be harmed or destroyed, and He has no name or desire.
God is the conqueror of all and is present everywhere and in every being. -61-
Tera Jor, Chachri Chhand (*Name and Style of Verses*)
God is present in water.
God is present on land.
God is fearless.
God's secrets cannot be known. -62-

God is Master of all.
God is perpetual and steady.
God has no particular abode.
God has no particular dress. -63-

Bhujangjang Prayat Chhand (*Name and Style of Verses*)
God's depth is unknown.
God is the source and embodiment of joy.
Salutations to God, to Whom all bow.
God is the Treasure of all. -64-

Salutations to God, Who has no master.
Salutations to God, who can destroy all.
Salutations to God, who cannot be defeated.
Salutations to God, Who can't be harmed. -65-

Salutations to God, Who can't be touched by death.
Salutations to God, Who does not need any
protection.
Salutations to God, Who is present everywhere.
Salutations to God, Who is present in every form.
-66-
Salutations to God, Who is King of Kings.
Salutations to God, Who created the entire creation.
Salutations to God, Who is the Emperor of emperors.
Salutations to God, Who gives light to the moon. -67-

Salutations to God, Who is the True Song.
Salutations to God, Who is the True Love.
Salutations to God, under Whose Will the world
functions.
Salutations to God, Who can cause everything to dry
up (end). -68-

Salutations to God, Who causes death of living
beings.
Salutations to God, Who enjoys the creation.
Salutations to God, Who conquers all.
Salutations to God, Who causes awe and fear in
everybody. -69-

Salutations to God, Who knows everything.
Salutations to God, Who created the universe.
Salutations to God, Whose Name is the greatest
magic.
Salutations to God, Whose name is the greatest
amulet. -70-

Salutations to God, Who watches everything.

Salutations to God, Who attracts all.
Salutations to God, Who is present in every color.
Salutations to God, Who can destroy everything. -71-

Salutations to God, Who is the source of life.
Salutations to God, Who is the Primal Seed (root of everything).
No one can cause any trouble to God, Who does everything, yet remains detached.
God confers boons on all. -72-

God is the fountain of compassion, and destroyer of sins.
God is the source of all spiritual and miraculous powers. -73-

Charpat Chhand (*Name of Verses*), **Tav Prasad** (*uttered with God's Grace*).
God's works are permanent.
God's Laws are Just.
The creation is attached to God.
God is the abode of permanent joy. -74-

The Kingdom of God is permanent.
God's creation is permanent (as per His Will).
God's Laws are perfect.
God's creation is beyond comprehension. -75-

God is the Giver of all.
God knows everyone's mind.
God gives light to all.
God is worshipped by all. -76-

God is the breath of all.
God is the shelter of all.
God is the enjoyer of all.
God is connected to all. -77-

God is worshipped by all Angels.
God knows the condition of all.
God can destroy all.
God nourishes all. -78-

Rual Chhand (*Name of Verses*), **Tav Prasad**
(*uttered with God's Grace*).

God existed before creation,
His origin is untraceable.
He does not take birth and is present everywhere.
All beings bow to God,
Who is the Supreme Light;
Worshipped by all, and Who is the origin of all.
God, the source of all tastes and pleasures is present
everywhere. -79-

God does not have any particular Name; He no form,
color or shape.
God, the Primal Creator, is present in all; He is not
born and exists forever.
God has no particular country, no shape, outline and
desire.
God is present in every place, and His Love is present
everywhere. -80-

God has no particular Name, or any visible abode.

All living beings bow before God, Who is worshipped everywhere.

God is One, but His manifestations are countless.

After enacting the world drama (creation), He packs up (ends the creation), and is all by Himself again. -81-

The secrets of God are unknown to divine beings and scriptures.

God has no shape, color or lineage, and no one can describe Him.

God has no parents and is beyond births and deaths.

Sometimes God appears as the Destroyer, and living beings are humbled by Him. -82-

In the fourteen worlds (everywhere), the Name of God is being repeated and remembered.

God is the original Divine Being and Symbol of Worship, Who created everything, everywhere.

God is the Supreme Power, is complete in all respects, and present in all.

God is the Creator of the entire universe; He is self-created; He creates and destroys the creation. -83-

God is beyond death and timeless, and belongs to no particular place.

God is the source of truth and virtues, is not visible and has no particular dress.

God has no form, no body, no color, no caste or name.

God humbles the vain, destroys the evil; He confers salvation and fulfills desires. -84-

God is self-created and beyond description;

His virtues cannot be fully narrated; He is Unique.
God smashes the pride of the sinners, and destroys them.
God existed since the beginning and is detached.
God has no body or soul, and is present in all.
God nurses and destroys all, God is capable of doing everything. -85-

God approaches all, destroys all, and is distinct from all.
None of the religious scriptures know of God's form, color or mark.
The Vedas and Puranas (ancient Hindu scriptures) declare that God is the Highest of all and there is none like Him.
Even by reading all the Holy Scriptures, one still cannot understand God completely. -86-

Madubhar Chhand (*Name of Verses*), **Tav Prasad** (*uttered with God's Grace*).
God is the source of all virtues, His benevolence is infinite.
His abode is perpetual.
No one possesses as many excellences as God. -87-

God is self-illuminated.
God is indestructible.
God controls all the Creation.
His is the Emperor of emperors. -88-

God is the King of kings.
God is the Sun of suns.

God is above all divine forms.
His praises are unlimited. -89-

God is the King of Indra (God of Weather).
He is the Highest of the high.
He is present with the poorest.
Death works by His Command. -90-

God is not made of elements.
God's Light is unending.
God cannot be measured.
His Excellences are countless. -91-

All Holy men bow before God.
He is free from fear and desires.
God is the Supreme Light.
No one can diminish His Grandeur. -92-

God's Works are performed effortlessly.
His Laws are Just.
God is the source of all beauty.
None can correct Him. -93-

Chachri Chhand (*Name of Verses*), **Tav Prasad**
(*uttered with God's Grace*).
God is The Nurturer, The Giver of salvation;The
Biggest Donor, and is Limitless. -94-

God Destroys. God Creates.
God has no particular name or temptation. -95-

Bhujang Prayat Chhand (*Name of Verses*)
God creates the entire Creation.

God destroys the entire Creation.
God showers His gifts to the entire creation.
God knows everything in the entire creation. -96-

God is present in the entire creation.
God nurtures all beings in the entire creation.
God protects all beings in the entire creation.
God destroys all beings in the entire creation. -97-

God resides everywhere in the entire creation.
God is present everywhere in the entire creation.
God is worshipped everywhere.
God gives to the entire creation. -98-

Chachri Chhand (*Name of Verses*)
God has no enemy, God has no friend.
God has no doubts, and is afraid of nobody. -99-

God is free from Karmas (actions). God has no body.
God is not born. God does not reside in any particular
place. -100-

God has no looks. God has no friend.
God is detached from all.
God is pure. -101-

God is the Master of the entire creation.
God existed from the beginning.
God is invisible.
God never becomes weak. -102-

Bhagwati Chhand (*Name of Verses*), **Tav Prasad
Kathate** (*uttered with God's Grace*).

20

God's abode is everywhere.
God's form is indestructible.
God cannot be attained by rituals.
God is free from all doubts. -103-

God's abode is permanent.
God can destroy the sun.
Mammon cannot influence God.
God is the source of wealth and honor. -104-

God's glory gives glory to the rulers.
God is the protector of justice.
God has no worries.
God is the Ornament of all. -105-

God is the Creator of the universe.
God is the bravest of the brave.
God is the most beautiful of all.
His is the essence of divine knowledge. -106-

God, Who is above all divine beings, existed from the
beginning.
God is self-illuminated.
No one can draw a picture if God.
God is the Controller of Himself. -107-

God gives nourishment to all.
God is merciful, and grants liberation.
God is pure and stainless.
God is invisible. -108-

God forgives sins.
God is the Emperor if emperors.
God is the Doer of everything.
God gives nourishment to all. -109-

God nurtures and is merciful on all.
God showers His gifts on all.
God is the Owner of all powers.
God is the Destroyer of all. -110-

God is worshipped everywhere.
God showers His gifts on all, everywhere.
God reaches all places.
God is present in all creation. -111-

God is present in every land.
God is manifested everywhere in different ways.
God is the King of His creation.
God gives glory to all. -112-

God confers gifts to all in every place.
God is present everywhere.
God's glory is present everywhere.
God's Light spreads everywhere. -113-

God is present in every land.
God is manifested in various ways.
God causes death to all.
God takes care of all. -114-

God enjoys all at every place.
God can reach everywhere.
God manifests in different forms everywhere.

22

God cares for all at every place. -115-

God's work is performed everywhere.
He is present as the Supreme Ruler everywhere.
He causes destruction everywhere.
He nurses all, everywhere. -116-

God's power is everywhere.
God is the breath of all.
God is present in every land.
God can be seen manifested in many ways. -117-

God is worshipped everywhere.
His is the Supreme Controller of the entire creation.
God is remembered everywhere.
God is present everywhere. -118-

God gives light to the Sun.
God is worshipped everywhere.
God is the King of all.
God gives light to the moon. -119-

God resides within all living beings.
God possesses Supreme Wisdom.
God is the fountain of learning.
God is the creator of languages. -120-

God is the embodiment of beauty.
All look towards God.
God exists forever.
No one can diminish the ever-lasting beauty of God's
creation. -121-

God causes the defeat of the evil.
God protects the innocent.
God's place is the Highest.
God is present in the world at all times -122-

God knows everything.
God takes care of all.
God is the greatest friend.
God gives food to all. -123-

God manifests in countless ways.
No one knows God's secret and he cannot be destroyed.
God protects the true devotees.
God punishes the evil doers. 124-

No one can portray God.
His Glory is above all.
All living beings are the Light of God.
God is the Supreme Nectar, present in all. -125-

God exists eternally.
He has no rivals.
God conquers all.
God is the Creator of the entire universe. -126-

God is honored by all.
God does not have any desire. No one can stand in the way of God.
God is unfathomable and has no equal. -127-

God existed before creation started.

God is the Light of all beings.
God has no body and name.
God runs the three worlds (creation). -128-

God is the Treasure of all.
God cannot be conquered and he is very deep.
God is the beauty present in all forms.
God loves all. -129-

The source of joy for all living beings is God.
God never becomes old and cannot be touched.
God can destroy hell.
God is pervading the entire creation. -130-

God's glory cannot be depicted.
God is ever present.
All get joy from God.
God is without an equal and is present in all. -131-

No one can describe the form of God.
All living beings are the light of God.
God's form is beyond description.
God is connected to all. -132-

Chachri Chhand (*Name of Verses*)
God is Indestructible. He has no limbs (body parts).
He has no dress. He is beyond description. -133-

He has no doubts. He is beyond rituals.
He has no beginning. He existed even before the ages
began -134-

He cannot be conquered. He cannot be destroyed.

He is not made of elements. He is unshakeable. -135-

He is perpetual. He is not entangled.
He is not attached to anything. He is beyond all
restraints. -136-

He is indifferent to love. He has no attachment.
He is beyond death. He is the supreme light -137-

He is carefree. He exists continuously. He cannot be
depicted. He cannot be seen. -138-

No can draw His portrait. He has no costumes.
He cannot be vanquished. He is unfathomable. -139-

He is incomprehensible. He is beyond reach.
He has no color. His origin is unknown. -140-

He is Unique.
He has existed forever.
He is beyond births.
He is completely free. -141-

Charpat Chhand, Tav Prasad (*Name of Verses,
uttered with God's Grace*).
God can kill all.
He can reach all.
He is known to all.
He knows all. -142-

He destroys all.
He creates all.
He is the breath and life of all.

He gives power to all. -143-

God causes all things to be done.
He gives virtues to all.
He is present in all.
He is separate from all. -144-

Rasaval Chhand, Tav Prasad (*Name of Verses, uttered with God's Grace*).
I bow to God Who destroys Hell (suffering).
His Light is forever.
He has no bodily form.
His light never fades. -145-
He destroys those who cause suffering to others.
He accomplishes everything.
He is boundless.
No one can stop His Light. -146-

God is formless and has no special name.
He is the Cherisher as well as the Destroyer of the three worlds (everything).
He cannot be destroyed.
There is none like Him. -147-

He has no grandson or son.
He has no enemy or friend.
He has no father or mother.
He has no caste or dynasty. -148-

He has no relatives or anyone.
He and His extent cannot be measured.
His Light is continuous.
He cannot be defeated and is beyond birth. -149-

Bhagvati Chhand, Tav Prasad (*Name of Verses, uttered with God's Grace*).
His Light is pervading everywhere.
He is present everywhere.
He is eternal.
Everyone sings His virtues. -150-
He is the most wise and intelligent.
He is the essence of all Beauty and Light.
He is merciful to all.
He takes pity and gives sustenance to all. -151-

He provides good for all.
He can confer salvation.
He is most bountiful.
He is most beautiful. -152-

He overpowers enemies.
He is the supporter of the poor.
He destroys enemies.
He destroys fear. -153-

He removes curses.
He lives in all.
No one can win Him.
He provides sustenance and is merciful -154-

God is the speech of all.
He is the most grand.
He can destroy hell.
He resides in heaven. -155-

He reaches out to all.

He is the source of all pleasures.
He looks after all.
All love Him. -156-

He is The Lord of Lords.
He is The Lord of all, forever.
He has no particular abode.
He has no particular dress. -157-

He is present on earth and in heaven.
God's mystery is great.
His bounties are wonderful.
He is the embodiment of beauty and bravery. -158-

His Light is perpetual
His smell is the most pleasant.
His beauty is a wonder.
His grandeur cannot be measured. -159-

He spreads everywhere.
He is the Light of the Soul.
He is steady and has no body.
He is boundless and imperishable. -160-

Madhubar Chhand, Tav Prasad (*Name of Verses, uttered with God's Grace*).
Holy saints bow with devotion before God.
He is the source of all virtues.
No one can defeat Him.
He is The Lord of all and capable of destroying everything.
-161-

All living beings salute God.
Saints worship Him in their minds.
His is the Emperor of all mortals.
God is complete in all respects. -162-

God is Indestructible.
He is the light and knowledge of the saints.
God's Light shines within the saints.
Salutations to God, Who has countless virtues.
Salutations to God, who is ever present in water and land. -163-

God never becomes old.
God's seat is everlasting.
No one is equal to God.
No one can describe God's Greatness. -164-

God is present in all waters and lands.
God is present everywhere,
God is Supreme on lands and seas.
God is present in countless forms at every place. -165-

God is Indestructible.
God is The Lord of all.
God is the Controller of all.
God is always One. -166-

God is present everywhere and does not change.
God's origin cannot be known through discourses.
God destroys evil in an instant.
God is Almighty and Immortal. -167-

His is worshipped in every house.
God's Holy Name resides in every heart.
God never becomes old.
God does not depend on anybody for anything. -168-

God is forever steady.
God's acts are free from anger.
God's stores are inexhaustible.
God was not created by anyone. -169-

God's Laws and Works are Just.
God's works are performed without fear.
No one can injure God.
His is the grandest donor of all. -170-

Har-Bol-Mana Chhand, Tav Prasad (*Name of Verses, uttered with God's Grace*).
God is Merciful.
God is the Destroyer of evil.
God is the slayer of evil doers.
God gives beauty to creation. -171-

God is the Owner of the creation.
God is the Master of all.
Wars start by the Will of God.
God is the savior of all. -172-

God is the Support of the earth.
God is the Creator of the universe.
God is in all hearts and minds.
All try to know God. -173-

God nourishes all.

God creates all.
God is close to all.
God destroys all. -174-

God is Compassionate.
God nurtures the world.
God is the Master of all.
God is the Owner of the creation. -175-

God is the Lord of the Universe.
God is the Destroyer of evil doers.
God is the biggest of all.
God is the essence of compassion. -176-

God is beyond words.
God cannot be installed at any particular place.
God's statue cannot be made.
God is the Divine Nectar and is Immortal. -177-

God is the Divine Nectar and is Eternal.
God is the fountain of Mercy.
God's image cannot be made.
God is the supporter of the earth. -178-

God is the source of the Divine Nectar.
God is the biggest Lord of all.
God's image cannot be made.
God is the Divine Nectar and is Immortal. -179-

God's form is wonderful.
God is the Divine Nectar and is Immortal.
God is the Master if men.
God is the destroyer of enemies. -180-

32

God nurtures the world.
God is the abode of mercy.
God is the Master of kings.
God is the Protector of all. -181-

God stops the cycle of transmigration.
God conquers enemies.
God corrects the evil.
God makes others repeat His Name. -182-

God is free from blemishes.
God is complete in every way.
God is the Creator of creators.
God is the destroyer of destroyers. -183-

God is the Primal Soul.
All souls originate from God.
God is the Controller of Himself
God's glory surpasses all glories. -184-

Bhujang Prayat Chhand, (*Name of Verses*)
Salutations to God, Who gives Light to the sun and moon.
Salutations to God, Who is the King of Indra (god of weather).
Salutations to God, who creates complete darkness, as well as the most brilliant light.
Salutations to God, who is the biggest of all beings and the origin of all -185-

Salutations to God, Who created the three qualities of *Rajogoon* (worldly attachment), *Tamogoon* (darkness of mind and evil), *Satogoon* (Truth and Peace).
Salutations to God, Who is the Primal Being and beyond the elements
Salutations to God, Who is the origin of all holy men and knowledge.
Salutations to God, Who is the greatest charm and magic, and Whose meditation is the highest form of meditation. -186-

Salutations to God, Who vanquishes enemies in war, and Who is the spring of the Highest Knowledge.
Salutations to God, Who infuses energy into good and water.
Salutations to God, by Whose command, disputes arise and then peace prevails.
Salutations to God, who is the King of all divine creations, and the source of Whose Grandeur is unknown. -187-

Salutations to God, Who is flawless and Who gives beauty to beautiful things.

Salutations to God, the fulfiller of hopes, Who is most Wonderful.
God has no body, is Indestructible, and His names are many.
God can destroy the entire creation if He Wills, and God is Eternal, without any form, and free from desires. -188-

Ek Achhari Chhand *(Name of Verse)*

34

God is Invincible. God is Indestructible.
God is Fearless. God is Immortal. -189-

God was never born. God is Everlasting.
God is Indestructible. God pervades everywhere. -
190-

God is Invincible. God is Indivisible.
God cannot be seen. God has no wants or desires. -
191-

God is beyond Time. God is the Home of
Compassion.
God's portrait cannot be drawn. God has no dress. -
192-

God has no particular Name. His has no desires.
God is Unfathomable. God cannot be damaged. -193-

God has no Master. God can destroy all.
God is not subject to births and deaths. God does not
observe silence (rituals). -194-

God is beyond Love. God has no color.
God has no form. God has no quoit. -195-

God is above good or bad deeds. God is free from
doubts.
God cannot be conquered. No one can draw a picture
of God. -196-

Bhujang Prayat Chhand (*Name of Verses*)

Salutations to Respected God, Who is the Destroyer of all.
Salutations to God, Who is Invincible, Who has no particular Name, and Who lives in all beings.

Salutations to God Who is unaffected by any desire, and Whose form can be seen in all beings.
God is the Destroyer of sins, and His Works are in accordance with His Laws. -197-

God is the Truth and source of knowledge and joy, and destroys evil.
God bestows blessings, creates and resides in all.
God's grandeur is wonderful and He causes havoc on foes (sinners).
God can destroy and create, and he confers gifts and Mercy to all.-198-

God is present in the entire creation, and His Divine Laws controls the creation.
God's Light is Everlasting, He is resplendent and present in all beings.
God destroys the misery of births and deaths, and is the embodiment of mercy and compassion.
God is Present in All, and His Grandeur will never diminish. -199-

Completed, Translation of Jaap Sahib

Jaap Sahib Transliteration

Ek Ongkar Satguru Parsad

Jaap

Sri mukhvakh patshahi dasvih.

Chhapai Chaand. Tav Parsad

Chakr chihan ar baran jatt ar pat nahin jeh.

Roop rang aur rekh bhekh kou keh na sakat keh.

Achal murat anbhau prakas amitoj kahijeh.

Kot indr indran sah sahan ganijai.

Tribhavan mahip sur nar asur, nate nate ban trin kahat.

Tav sarab Nam kathai kavan, karam Nam barnat sumat. -1-

Bhujang Prayat Chhand

Namastwang akale. Namastwang kripale.

Namastang arupe. Namastang anupe. -2-

Namastang abhekhe. Namastang alekhe.

Namastang akaeh. Namastang ajae. -3-

Namastang aganje. Namastang abhanje.

Namastang aname. Namastang athame. -4-

Namastang akarmang. Namastang adharmang.

Namastang anamang. Namastang adhamang. -5-

Namastang ajite. Namastang abhite.

Namastang abahe. Namastang adhahe. -6-

Namastang anile. Namastang anade.

Namastang achhede. Namastang agadhe. -7-

Namastang aghanje. Namastang abhanje.

Namastang udare. Namastang apare. -8-

Namastang su ekai. Namastang anekai.

Namastang abhute. Namastang ajupe. -9-

Namastang nrikarme. Namastang nribharme.

Namastang nridese. Namastang nribhese. -10-

Namastang nriname. Namastang nrikame.

Namastang nridhate. Namastang nrighate. -11-

Namastang nridhute. Namastang abhute.

Namastang aloke. Namastang asokeh. -12-

38

Namastang nritapeh. Namastang athape.

Namastang trimane. Namastang nidhane. -13-

Namastang agahe. Namastang abahe.

Namastang tribargeh. Namastang asargeh. -14-

Namastang prabhoge. Namastang sujoge.

Namastang arange. Namastang abhange. -15-

Namastang aganmeh. Namastast ranmeh.

Namastang jalasreh. Namastang nirasreh. -16-

Namastang ajate. Namastang apateh.

Namastang amajbeh. Namastast ajbeh. -17-

Adesang adeseh. Namastang abhese.

Namastang nridhameh. Namastang nribameh. -18-

Namo sarab kaleh. Namo sarab dialeh.

Namo sarab roopeh. Namo sarab bhupeh. -19-

Namo sarab khapeh. Namo sarab thape.

Namo sarab kaleh. Namk sarab paleh. -20-

Namastast devai. Namastang abhevai.

Namastang ahanmeh. Namastang subanmeh. -21-

Namo sarab gauneh. Namo sarab bhaune.

Namo sarab rangeh. Namo sarab bhange. -22-

Namo kal kale. Namastast diale.

Namastang abharneh. Namastang amarneh. -23-

Namastang jrarang. Namastang kritarang.

Namo sarab dhandhe. Namo sat abandhe. -24-

Namastang nrisakeh. Namastang nribakeh.

Namastang rahimeh. Namastang karimeh. -25-

Namastang anante. Namastang mahante.

Namastast rage. Namastang suhage. -26-

Namo sarab sokhang. Namo sarab pokhang.

Namo sarab karta. Namo sarab harta. -27-

Namo jog jogeh. Namo bhog bhogeh.

Namo sarab dialeh. Namo sarab paleh. -28-

Chachri Chand. Tav Prasad

Arup hain. Anup hain. Aju hain. Abhu hain. -29-

Alekh hai. Abhekh hain. Anam hain. Akam hain. -30-

Adhe hain. Abhe hain. Ajit hain. Abhit hain. -31-

Triman hain. Nidhan hain. Tribargh haim. Asarg hain. -32-

Anil hain. Anad hain. Ajeh hain. Ajad hain. -33-

Ajanam haim. Abarn haim. Abhut hain. Abharn hain. -34-

Aganj hain. Abhanj hain. Ajhujh hain. Ajhanjh hain. -35-

Amik hain. Rafik hain. Adhandh hain. Abandh hain. -36-

Nribujh hain. Asujh hain. Akal hain. Ajal hain -37-

Alah hain. Ajah hain. Anant hain. Mahant hain -38-

Alik hain. Nrisrik hain. Nrilambh hain. Asambh hain. -39-

Aganm hain. Ajanm hain. Abhut hain. Achhut hain. -40-

Alok hain. Asok hain. Akarm hain. Abharm hain. -41-

Ajit hain. Abhit hain. Abah hain. Agah hain. -42-

Amaan hain. Nidhan hain. Anek hain. Phir ek hain. -43-

Bhujang Prayat Chhand

Namo sarab maane. Samasti nidhane.

Namo dev deveh. Abhekhi abheve. -44-

Namo kal kaleh. Namo sarab paleh.

Namo sarab gaune. Namo sarab bhaune. -45-

Anangi anathe. Nrisangi pramathe.

Namo bhan bhane. Namo maan maaneh. -46-

Namo chandr chandre. Namo bhan bhane.

Namo git gite. Namo taan taneh. -47-

Namo nrit nritte. Namo naad nadeh.

Namo paan paneh. Namo baad badeh -48-

Anangi aname. Samasti sarupeh.

Prabhangi pramatheh. Samasti bibhute. -49-

Kalankang bina nekalanki sarupe.

Namo raj rajeswarang param roopeh. -50-

Namo jog jogeswarang param siddhe.

Namo raj rajeswarang param bridhe. -51-

Namo sastarpaneh. Namo astarmaneh.

Namo param giata. Namo lok mata. -52-

Abhekhi abhanni, abhogi abhuge.

Namo jog jogeswarang param jugte. -53-

Namo nitt naraene, kruer karme.

Namo pret apret, deve sudharme. -54-

Namo rog harta, namo raag rupeh.

Namo shah shahang, namo bhup bhupe. -55-

Namo daan daneh, namo maan maneh.

Namo rog rogeh, namastang snane. -56-

Namo mantr mantrang. Namo jantr jantrang.

Namo ist iste. Namo tantr tantrang. -57-

Sada sacch danand sarbang pranasi.

Anupe arupe, samastul nivasi. -58-

Sada sidhida bhudhida bridh karta.

Adho urdh ardhang aghang ogh harta. -59-

Parang param parmeswarang prochh-palang.

Sada sarabda sidh data dialang. -60-

Achhedi abhedi, anamang akamang.

Samasto paraji samastast dhamang. -61-

Tera Jor. Chachri Chhand

Jale hain. Thale hain. Abhit hain. Abhe hain. -62-

Prabhu hain. Aju hain. Ades hain. Abhes hain. -63-

Bhujang Prayat Chhand

Aghade abadhe. Anandi sarupe

Namo sarab maneh. Samasti nidhane. -64-

Namastwang nrinathe. Namastwang pramathe.

Namastwang aganje. Namastwang abhanje. -65-

Namastwang akale. Namastwang apale.

Namo sarab dese. Namo sarab bhese. -66-

Namo raj raje. Namo saj saje.

Namo shah shahe. Namo mah mahe. -67-

Namo git gite. Namo prit prite.

Namo rokh rokhe. Namo sokh sokhe. -68-

Namo sarab roge. Namo sarab bhoge.

Namo sarab jitang. Namo sarab bhitang. -69-

Namo sarab gianang. Namo param tanang.

Namo sarab mantrang. Namo sarab jantrang. -70-

Namo sarab drissang. Namo sarab krissang.

Namo sarab range. Tribhangi anange. -71-

Namo jiv jivang. Namo bij bije.

Akhijje abhije. Samastang prasijje. -72-

Kripalang sarupe, kukarmang pranasi.

Sada sarabda nidh sidhang nivasi. -73-

Charpat Chhand. Tav Prasad

Amrit karme. Abrit dharme.

Akhall joge. Achall bhoge. -74-

Achall raje. Atall saje.

Akhall dharmang. Alakhkarmamg. -75-

Sarbang data. Sarbhang giata.

Sarbhang bhane. Sarbhang maneh. -76-

Sarbang pranang. Sarbhang tranang.

Sarbang bhugta. Sarbjang jugta. -77-

Sarbang devang. Sarbang bhevang.

Sarbhang kaleh. Sarbhang paleh. -78-

Rual Chhand. Tav Prasad

Aad roop anaad murat, ajon purakh apar.

Sarab maan trimaan dev, abhev aad udar.

Sarab palak sarab ghalak, sarab ko poon kal.

Jattta tattra birajhi, avdhut roop rasal. -79-

Nam tham na jat jakar, roop rung na rekh.

Ad purakh udar murat, ajon ad asekh.

Des aur na bhes jakar, roop rekh na raag.

Jattra tattra disa visah, hoey phaileo anurag. -80-

Nam kam bihin pekhat, dham hoon naih jah.

Sarab maan sarbattra maan, sadaiv manat tahi.

Ek murat anek darshan, kin roop anek.

Khel khel akhel khelan, antt ko phir ek. -81-

Dev bhev na janhi, jeh bedh aur kateb.

Roop rung na jaat paat, su jani keh jeb.

Tatt matt na jat jakar, janam maran bihin.

Chakkra bakkra phirai chatur chakk manhi pur teen. -82-

Lok chaudah ke bikhai, jag japhi jeh jaap.

Aad dev anaad murat, thapio sahai jeh thaap.

Param roop punit moorar, puran purakh apar.

Sarab bisv rachio suyambhav, garan bhanjanhar. -83-

Kal hin kala sanjugat, akal purakh ades.

Dharam dham su bharam rehat, abhut alakh abhes.

Ang raag na rang jakaih, jat path na nam.

Garab ganjan dust bhanjan, mukat daik kam. -84-

Ap roop amik an ustat, ek purakh avdhut.

Garab ganjan sarab bhanjan, ad roop asoot.

Ang hin abhang anatam, ek purakh apar.

Sarab lail, sarab ghaik, sarab ko pratipar. -85-

Sarab ganta sarab janta, sarab te anbhekh

sarab sastr na jan-hi, jeh roop rung ar rekh

Param bedh puraan jakaih, net bhakhat nitt.

Kot sinmirat puran sastr. Na avii wihchitt. -86-

Madhubhar Chaand, Tav Prasad

Goon gan udar. Mehma apaar.

Asan abhang. Upma anang. -87-

Anbhau prakas. Nisdin anas.

Ajan bah. Shahan shah. -88-

Rajan raj. Bhanan bhan.

Devan dev. Upma mahan. -89-

Indran Indr. Balan bal.

Rankan runk. Kalan kal. -90-

Anbhut ang.Abha abhang.

Gat mit apar. Gun gan udar. -91-

Mun gan pranam. Nirbhai nikam.

Att dut prachand. Mit gat akhand. -92-

Alisya karam. Adrisya dharam.

Sarba bharnadhya. Andand badhya. -93-

Chachri Chhand. Tav Prasad

Gubinde. Mukande. Udare. Apare. -94-

Hariang. Kariang. Nriname. Akame. -95-

Bhujang Prayat Chhand

Chattra chakkra karta. Chattra chakkra harta.

Chattra chakkra daneh. Chattra chakkra janeh. -96-

Chattra chakkra varti. Chattra chakkra bhanti.

Chattra chakkra paleh. Chattra chakkra kaleh. -97-

48

Chattra chakkra paseh. Chattra chakkra vaseh.

Chattra chakkra manyai. Chattra chakkra danyai. -98-

Chachri Chhand

Na sattrai. Na mittrai. Na bharmang. Ma bhittrai. -99-

Na karmang. Na kaeh. Ajanmanh. Ajaeh. -100-

Na chittrai. Na mittrai pareh hain. Pavittrai. -101-

Prithisai. Adisai. Adrisai. Akrisai. -102-

Bhagwati Chhand. Tav Prasad Kathate

Ke achhij desai. Ke abhijh bhesai.

Ke aganj karmai. Ke abhanj bharmai. -103-

Le abhij lokai. Ke adit sokai.

Ke avdhut barnai. Ke bibhut karnai. -104-

Ke rajang prabha hain. Ke dharmang dhuja hain.

Ke asok harnai. Ke sarba abharnai. -105-

Ke jagtang kriti hain. Ke chhatrang chhatri hain.

Ke brahamang sarupai. Ke anbhau anupai. -106-

Ke aad adev hain. Ke aap abhev hain.

Ke chittrang bihinai. Ke ekai adhinai. -107-

Ke rozi razakai. Rahimul rihakai.

Ke paik be-aib hain. Ke gaibul gain hain. -108-

Ke afual gunah hain. Ke shahan shah hain.

Ke karan kunind hain. Ke rozi dihand hain. -109-

Ke razak rahim hain. Ke karmang karim hain.

Ke sarbang kali hain.

Ke sarbang dali hain. -110-

Ke sarbattra manayai. Ke sarbattra danayai.

Ke sarbattra gaunai. Ke sarbattra bhaunai. -111-

Ke sarbattra desai. Ke sarbattra bhesai.

Ke sarbattra rajai. Ke sarbattra sajai. -112-

Ke sarbattra dinai. Ke sarbattra linai

Ke sarbattra jaho. Ke sarbattra bhaho. -113-

Ke sarbattra desai. Ke sarbattra bhesai.

Ke sarbattra kalai. Ke sarbattra palai. -114-

Ke sarbattra hanta. Ke sarbattra ganta.

Ke sarbattra bhekhi. Ke sarbattra pekhi. -115-

Ke sarbattra kajai. Ke sarbattra rajai.

Ke sarbattra sokhai. Ke sarbattra pokhai. -116-

Ke sarbattra tranai. Ke sarbattra pranai.

Ke sarbattra desai. Ke sarbattra bhesai. -117-

Ke sarbattra manayai. Sadaivang pradhanyai.

Ke sarbattra japayai. Ke sarbattra thapayai. -118-

Ke sarbattra bhanai. Ke sarbattra manai.

Ke sarbattra indrai. Ke sarbattra chandrai. -119-

Ke sarbang kalimai. Ke parmang fahimai.

Ke akal alamai. Ke sahib klamai. -120-

Heh husnul vaju hain. Tamamull ruju hain.

Hamesul slamai. Salikhat mudamai. -121-

Ganimull shikastai. Garibul prastai.

Bilandul makanai. Zaminul zamanai. -122-

Tamizul tamamai. Rujual nidhanai.

Hariful azimai. Razaik yakinai. -123-

Anekul trang hain. Abhed hain abhang hain.

Azizul nivaz hain. Ganimul khiraj hain. -124-

Nirukat saroop hain. Trimukat bibhut hain.

Prabhugat prabja hain. Sujugat sudha hain. -125-

Sadaivang saroop hain. Abhedi anoop hain.

Samasto paraj hain. Sada sarab saj hain. -126-

Samastul salam hain. Sadaivul akam hain.

Nribadh saroop hain. Agadh hain, Anoop hain. -127-

O'ang aad roope. Anad saroope.

Anangi aname. Tribhangi trikame. -128-

Tribargang tribadhe. Aganje agadhe.

Subhang sarab bhage. Su sarba anurage. -129-

Tribhigat saroop hain. Achhij hain acchut hain.

Ke narkang pranas hain. Prithiul pravas hain. -130-

Nirukat prabha hain. Sadaivang sada hain.

Bubhugat saroop hain. Prajugat anoop hain. -131-

Nirukat sada hain. Bibhugat prabha hain.

Anukat saroop hain. Prajugat anoop hain. -132-

Chachri Chaand

Abhang hain. Anang hain. Abhekh hain. Alekh hain. -133-

Abharm hain. Akarm hain. Anad hain. Jugad hain. -134-

Ajai haih. Abai hain. Abhit hai. Adhut hai. -135-

Anas hain. Udas hain. Adhandh hai. Abandh hain. -136-

Abhagat hain. Birakat hain. Anas hain. Prakas hain. -137-

Nichint hain. Sunint hain. Alikkh hain. Adikkh hain. -138-

Alekh hain. Abhekh hain. Adhah hain. Agah hain. -139-

Asanbh hain. Aghanb hain. Anil hain. Anad hain. -140-

Anitt hain. Sunitt hain. Ajat hain. Ajad hain. -141-

Charpat Chhand. Tav Prasad

Sarbang hanta. Sarbang ganta.

Sarbang khiata. Sarbang giata.-142-

Sarbang harta. Sarbang karta.

Sarbang pranang. Sarbang tranang. -143-

Sarbang karmang. Sarbang dharmang.

Sarbang jugta. Sarbang mukta. -144-

Rasaval Chhand. Tav Prasad.

Namo narak naseh. Sadaivang prakase.

Anangang sarupe. Abhangang bibhute. -145-

Pramathang pramathe. Sada sarab sathe.

Agadh sarupe. Nribadh bhibhute. -146-

Anangi aname. Tribhangi trikame.

Nribhangi sarupe. Sarbhangi anupe -147-

No potrai na puttrai. Na sattrai na mittrai.

Na tatai na matai. Na jatai na patai. -148-

Nrisakang sarik hain. Amito amik hain.

Sadaivang prabha hain. Ajai hain aja hain. -149-

Bhagvati Chhand. Tav Prasad

Ke zahar zahur hain. Ke hazar hazur hain.

Hamesul salam hain. Samastul kalam hain. -150-

He sahib dimag hain. He husnul charag hain.

Ke kamal karim hain. Ke razak rahim hain. -151-

Ke rozi dihind hain. Ke razak rahind hain.

Karimul kamal hain. Ke husnul jamal hain. -152-

Ganimul khiraj hain. Garibul nivaz hain.

Hariful shikann hain. Hirasul fikann hain -153-

Kalankang pranas hain. Samastul nivas hain.

Aganjul ganim hain. Razaik rahim hain -154-

Samastul zuban hain. Ke sahib kiran hain.

Ke narkang pranas hain. Bahistul nivas hain. -155-

Ke sarbul gavann hain. Hamesul ravann hain.

Tamamul tamiz hain. Samastul aziz hain. -156-

Parang param iss hain. Samastul adis hain.

Adesul alekh hain. Hamesul abhekh hain. -157-

Zaminul zaman haim. Amikul iman hain.

Karimul kamal hain. Ke juratt jamal hain. -158-

Ke achlang prakas hain. Ke amito subas hain.

Ke ajab sarup hain. Ke amito bibhut hain. -159-

Ke amito pasa hain. Ke atam prabha hain.

Ke achlang anang hain. Ke amito abhang hain. -160-

Madubhar Chhand, Tav Prasad

Mun mann pranam. Goon gan mudam.

Ar bar aganj. Har nar prabhanj. -161-

An gan pranam. Moon mann salam.

Har nar akhand. Bar nar amand. -162-

Anbhav anas. Moon mann prakas.

Goon gan pranam. Jal thal mudam. -163-

Anchij ang. Asan abhang.

Upma apaar. Gat mitt udar. -164-

Jal thal amand. Dis vis abhand.

Jal thal mahant. Dis vis beant. -165-

Anbhav anas. Dhrit dhar dhuras.

Ajan bah. Ekai sadah. -166-

Onkar adh. Kathni anaad.

Khal khand khial. Gurbar akaal.-167-

Ghar ghar pranam. Chit charan naam.

Anchijj gat. Ajij na baat. -168-

Anjhanj gat. Anranj baat.

Antut bhandar. Anthat apaar. -169-

Adith dharam. Att dhith karam.

Anbran anant. Data mahant. -170-

Har Bol-Manna Chhand. Tav Prasad

Karunalya hain. Arr ghalya hain

Khal khandan hain. Maih mandan hain. -171-

Jagtesvar hain. Parmeswar hain.

Kal karan hain. Sarab ubaran hai. -172-

Dhrit ke dhran hain. Jag ke kran hain.

Mann maniya hain. Jag janiya hain -173-

Sarbang bhar hain. Saebang kar hain.

Sarab pasiya hain. Sarab nasiya hain -174-

Karunakar hain. Bisvanbhar hain.

Sarbesvar hain. Jagtesvar hain. -175-

Brahmandas hain. Khal khandas hain.

Par teh par hIn. Karunakar hain. -176-

Ajapa jap hain. Athapa thap hain.

Akrita krit hain. Amrita mrit haim. -177-

Amrita mrit hain. Karuna krit hain.

Akrita krit hain. Dharni dhrit hain. -178-

Amitesvar hain. Parmesvar hain.

Akrita krit hain. Amrita mrit hain. -179-

Ajba krit hain. Amrita mrit hain

Nar naik hain. Khal ghaik hain. -180-

Bisvanbhar hain. Karunalya hain.

Nrip naik hain. Sarab paik hain. -181-

Bhav bhanjan hain. Ar ganjan hain.

Rip tapan hain. Japp japann hain. -182-

Aklang krit hain. Sarba krit hain

Karta kar hain. Harta har hain. -183-

Parmatam hain. Sarbatam hain.

Atam bas hain. Jas ke jas hain -184-

Bhujang Prayat Chhand

Namo suraj surje, namo chandr chandre.

Namo raj rajeh, namo Indr Indreh.

Namo andhkare, namo tej tejeh.

Namo brind brindeh, namo bij bijeh. -185-

Namo rajsang tamsang satt roope.

Namo param tattang atattang saroope.

Namo jogj jogeh, namo gian gianeh.

Namo mantr mantreh, namo dhian dhianeh. -186-

Namo judh judhe, namo gian gianeh.

Namo bhoj bhojeh, namo paan paneh.

Namo kalah karta, namo santt roope.

Namo Indr Indreh, anadang bibhuteh. -187-

Kalankar roope, alankar alanke.

Namo aas aseh, namo baank banke.

Abhangi saroope, anangi anaameh.

Tribhangi trikale, anangi akaame. -188-

Ek Acchari Chhand

Ajai. Alai. Abhai. Abai. -189-

Abhu. Ajoo. Anaas. Akaas. -190

Aganj. Abhanj. Alakkh. Abhakkh. -191-

Akal. Diaal. Alekh. Abhekh. -192-

Anaam. Akaam. Agah. Adhah. -193-

Anatheh. Pramatheh. Ajoni. Amoni -194-

Na raageh. Na rangeh. Na roopeh. Na rekheh. -195-

Akarmang. Abharmang. Aganjeh. Alekheh. -196-

Bhujang Prayat Chhand

Namastul pranameh, samastul pranaseh.

Aganjul anameh, samastul nivaseh.

Nrikamang bibhuteh, samastul sarupeh.

Kukarmang pranasi, sudharmang bibhuteh. -197-

Sada sacch danand sattrang pranasi.

Karimul kuninda, samastul nivasi.

Ajaib bibhuteh gajaib ganimeh.

Hariang kariang karimul rahimeh. -198-

Chattr chakkr varti, chattr chakkr bhugteh.

Suyambhav subhang sarabda sarab jugteh.

Dukalang pranasi dialang saroope.

Sada ang sangeh abhangang bibhute. -199-

Complete – GOD BLESS YOU and May You Always Be Happy

Made in the USA
Middletown, DE
08 January 2020

82814589R00036